PRACTICAL COMPANIONS

Kitchen
Gardener

by SUE PHILLIPS

Illustrated by ANNY EVASON

M·Q·P

Contents

CHAPTER ONE

Kitchen Garden Styles

Introduction

The first plant I ever grew was a giant summer marrow, which my grandfather and I drip-fed with sugar-water through a string in its stem, and which had my name scratched on it when it was just 1in (2.5cm) long. By the end of the summer it was 3ft (1m) long, too heavy to lift, and looked like an advertisement hoarding. I was just four at the time, but I've had a particular affection for edible gardening ever since.

Wherever I've lived, I've grown something to eat. I think a small self-sufficiency streak lies under the skin in most people, and there is nothing like starting in a small way to bring it out.

When I was a child, everyone we knew grew vegetables at the bottom of the garden. Ours was a neat patch occupying a quarter of the plot, where I remember pulling radishes and picking blackcurrants. The great attractions, from my point of view, were several huge fruit trees (ideal for climbing practice and tree-house camps), and the greasy, clay soil that made perfect pots when baked in the ashes of the bonfire. I'm sure it was this garden that set me on the road to a horticultural career.

The Manor House Garden

*I*n Victorian times, grand country houses were not complete without their walled kitchen gardens. Ruled with a rod of iron by the head gardener – the outdoor equivalent of the butler – these provided fruit and vegetables for the kitchens, and much more. Novelty crops, such as seakale and cardoon, which are rarely seen today, were Victorian favourites. Special green-houses were equipped to force out-of-season luxuries, such as grapes, figs, and peaches, plus exotics, such as pineapples. The kitchen garden also provided all the cut flowers and pot plants used for floral decoration in the house, and it was the gardeners who did the arrangements. The Victorian kitchen garden was, first and foremost, a status symbol. House guests would be escorted round the garden by their host so they could admire the magnificence of

 his domain. The traditional layout included a central path, flanked by extravagant flower borders, down which visitors promenaded, and which provided a decorative foreground to all the neat rows of vegetables and the scurrying staff beyond.

The Cottage Garden

*I*n contrast to the Lord of the Manor, rural Victorians, some of whom earned a meagre living tending his lordship's vast acres, had to make do with whatever tiny pieces of land surrounded their homes. The image depicted in Victorian watercolours of smiling mothers surrounded by old-fashioned cottage borders, and beatific children cuddling kittens among the hollyhocks, is an extremely idealised version of cottage life, and can be dismissed as romantic fantasy. In reality, vast numbers of Victorian countryfolk were obliged to live in squalor, and in many cases, the few meagre vegetables they were able to grow were all that stood between them and starvation.

Potagers

Potagers are a fashionable and decorative alternative to traditional kitchen gardens. The name comes from the grand, formal vegetable gardens of France, such as that at the Château Villandry, where a series of geometrically shaped beds, edged with boxwood, grow produce for the house. Potagers are easy to adapt to a more modest scale and, because they are so decorative, they are ideal for a small garden where crops cannot be hidden from view. A modern potager could incorporate flowers for cutting, a seat, deep or raised beds, and walls or trellises to support climbers, such as vines. Instead of boxwood, beds may be edged with tiles, clipped evergreen herbs, or rows of flowers, in keeping with the style of the rest of the garden.

Deep Beds

Having discovered the benefits of deep beds, I wouldn't consider growing vegetables in any other way. Cultivating the soil very deeply, and adding lots of well-rotted compost or manure allows roots to travel downwards instead of sideways for their water and nutrients. This means you can grow plants much closer together than you would in a conventional garden. You can reduce spacings by one third, and dispense altogether with paths between the rows, so you grow much more in the same space. Deep beds are less work too. Because the plants are grown close together, they soon fill the rows and smother out weeds, so less hoeing is needed. Plants grow better too, since the soil is never walked on, and stays uncompacted. All the work is done from the paths around the beds.

The Ornamental Kitchen Garden

I'm a passionate cottage gardener, and have long been fascinated by the idea of flowers and vegetables growing together in glorious disarray in my borders. Sadly, in reality, vegetables grown among flowers merely attract record numbers of slugs, and fail to make proper hearts, or reach full size, due to competition and shading from their floral neighbours. It is possible to compromise, by planting colourful varieties of popular vegetables, which are just as tasty as the green ones, in a decorative bed, or by growing flowers among complementary vegetables.

Patios and Balconies

*I*n gardens too tiny for a conventional kitchen garden, cultivate a pretty, potted version in containers. Choose a sunny, sheltered corner of the patio, and grow decorative crops, such as zucchini, sweet peppers, and aubergines. Grow pole beans, sugar snap peas, mange-tout, cucumbers, and outdoor tomatoes in tubs, and support their stems with ornamental pagodas or spires of bunched willow wands. Use tubs at the bases of pergola poles or trellises to grow kiwis or grape vines. Half-barrels are large enough to grow dwarf fruit trees – orange and lemon trees will thrive outdoors in summer, even in cooler regions. Save hanging baskets for tiny, trailing tomatoes, or a mixture of herbs.

The secret of success with potted kitchen gardens is water. As a general rule, the smaller the container, and the more plants it holds, the more often it will need watering – up to twice daily in hot summers. Regular feeding is vital if your potted kitchen garden is to produce tasty, tender crops. Use liquid tomato fertiliser, or an organic equivalent containing a good range of trace elements, which are essential for flavour, plus a liquid seaweed extract.

Indoor Gardens

*I*n cooler regions, you can grow exotic fruits in a conservatory. Opt for standard-trained citrus trees and potted figs, with passion fruit climbing up the walls and along the rafters, and miniature banana trees, and guavas in tubs. Try an olive tree, which naturally makes a craggy shape reminiscent of Mediterranean groves, or grow a grape vine trained as a standard tree – all gnarled trunk, and a leafy head dripping with fruits.

Windowsill

You can even have a vegetable garden indoors. I raise salad sprouts in jars, rinsing the seeds twice daily with clean water through cheesecloth (muslin) lids. Most varieties are ready to eat within a few days. Alfalfa (lucerne), tasting of fresh garden peas, is my favourite, and is also the fastest to grow. Setting the jars on a windowsill helps the sprouts to green up, which gives them the best flavour. Mung beans (Chinese bean sprouts) produce the largest crop, but I usually add a few fenugreek seeds for their tangy taste.

A kitchen windowsill makes a good winter herb garden. Pot up a few roots of mint, dug up from the garden. They should start sprouting in a few weeks. I raise herbs, such as flat-leaved parsley, chervil, and basil in pots. There is no need to thin out the seedlings or transplant to larger pots; start snipping as soon as they are big enough, then sow new pots when the old ones are half used.

Heirloom Vegetables

Some gardeners specialise in growing heirloom vegetables – old varieties that are rarely found in 'normal' seed catalogues. These have been saved from extinction by enthusiasts, because the vegetables have special attributes, such as taste, or appearance, that make them worth preserving. Today, a few seed suppliers specialise in heritage vegetables, and there are seed exchange schemes which you can join.

Early Rose Potato
Solanum tuberosum

Couve Tronchuda or Portugal Cabbage
Brassica oleracea var. *tronchuda*

Country gentleman (Shoepeg) Corn
Zea mays

Musselburgh Leek
Allium ampeloprasum

American Wonder Peas
Pesum satium

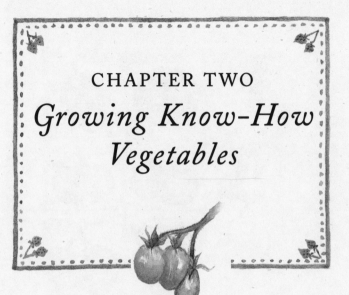

CHAPTER TWO
Growing Know-How
Vegetables

To grow healthy, succulent, tender vegetables, a good site is essential so the crops can grow quickly. Vegetables need plenty of light; the kitchen garden should be in sun for most of the day. (In light shade, only leafy crops, such as cabbages or lettuces, will do well.) Shelter is important too – strong winds can 'scorch' crops, or blow them over. The soil should be deep, rich, and fertile, full of organic matter to help retain moisture, and completely free of perennial weeds. Tough, stringy, or tasteless vegetables, or early bolting, are signs that the growing conditions are not right – rectify them, and all will be well.

Brassicas

*B*rassicas, which include Brussels sprouts, cabbages, cauli-flowers, and broccoli, must have firm soil – without it, they do not form proper hearts. With the exception of spring cabbages, which are sown in mid summer, brassicas should be sown in mid spring. You can buy-in plants, but you run the risk of importing root diseases into your garden on their roots, so grow your own from seed, if possible. Sow in an outdoor seed bed and transplant the seedlings to their final positions when they are a few inches (centimetres) high. For early crops in cooler regions, raise young plants in a green-house and plant out when the soil has warmed up. Spacings vary, depending on which brassicas you grow, but as a rough guide, plants should be spaced the same distances apart as their ultimate heights. Cauliflowers are tricky to grow and are notorious for running to seed in dry soil, so water them regularly. For small gardens try growing mini-cauliflowers. They produce 2-3in (5-8cm) heads within 3-4 months. You can speed up growth by watering the plants with a liquid fertiliser.

Onions and Leeks

*T*he easiest way to grow onions is by planting 'sets', which resemble small bulbs, in early spring. Press each set, blunt-end down, into the soil, and give a half turn to 'screw' it in place. Unless the base comes into contact with the soil, the set will not root. Plant garlic the same way, using the largest cloves separated from a large head, or buy cloves from a seed supplier. Easy to grow and tolerant of a wide range of soil types, leeks belong to the same family as onions. Grow them from seeds sown in spring in an outdoor seed bed. Thin them out to 1in (2.5cm) or more apart, then transplant the seedlings when they are large enough to handle. Grow leeks 4in (10cm) apart each way in deep beds, for tall white stems, or 12in (30cm) apart in rows 6in (15cm) apart in conventional plots, for larger plants. Leeks are ready to eat in autumn and winter. If a few plants run to seed, you can include the fluffy seedheads in dried flower arrangements.

Celery

Celery is regarded, even by seasoned vegetable growers, as a challenge. Plants are notoriously fickle, and will run to seed at the first opportunity. The right soil is essential. It must be deep, rich, and well manured – really packed with organic matter. To raise plants, sow seeds in seed trays of potting mix in a heated propagator at 60°F (15°C) in mid spring, and prick out the seedlings into individual pots when they are large enough to handle. Temperature is crucial at this stage. If it drops below 50°F (10°C) there is a good chance plants will bolt later, however good their growing conditions. If you don't have the facilities to grow from seed, buy pot-grown plants, and plant them out after the last frosts. Space them 12in (30cm) apart in rows 15in (40cm) apart, water well and feed regularly with nitrogen-rich liquid fertiliser – it is vital that the plants' growth is not checked, as they will bolt, or become tough and stringy. Dig them up in late summer or autumn, when they are large enough to use.

Asparagus

Asparagus plants are perennial, so instead of growing them in the vegetable garden, prepare a separate bed for them. Dig deeply, burying large quantities of rich organic matter. Seaweed is especially beneficial (asparagus does not mind small amounts of salt), or use seaweed meal from an organic gardening supplier. If the ground is well drained, asparagus will grow in a level bed. On wet, or clay soil, construct a raised bed 6in (15cm) or more above ground level, or plant on top of ridges in the traditional way. Asparagus plants are sold in early spring as dormant crowns – spread the roots out well, and plant in a shallow trench, covering them with 2in (5cm) of soil. As the season progresses, gradually hill up the plants until the trench is filled. Nurseries and garden centres sometimes sell pot-grown plants, and these are best planted in early summer. Choose all-male varieties, as these have thick, succulent stems. Feed and mulch asparagus beds heavily every spring. Don't cut any spears the year after planting. Take a few the next year, and slowly increase after that. Always allow the foliage to die down naturally in autumn.

Globe Artichoke

Globe artichokes are also perennials. If space is short, grow them in flower borders. Otherwise, make a separate bed for them in the kitchen garden. The plants resemble decorative thistles, with soft, spiky, silver-green foliage from which 4-5ft (12-15m) tall flower stems appear in summer. The edible part is the flower bud, which should be picked when tightly shut, and about the size of a fist. Plant offsets, or pot-grown plants in spring, 3ft (1m) apart each way, and water well. You can expect one or two heads the first year, but plants come into full cropping the second year. Cut suitable buds as they appear, with a few inches (centimetres) of stem. In autumn, cut down the stems and protect the crowns with straw. After four years, crowns are past their best – dig them up in early spring, separate the young offsets from the edge of the clump, and replant them in a new spot. The most popular artichokes are 'Vert de Laon', 'Green Glove' and 'Grand Cannes de Bretagne'.

Leafy Vegetables

Oriental greens, spinach and Swiss chard are all fast-growing, leafy crops, which need the same conditions as lettuces. High temperatures and dry soil can cause plants to bolt. Sow spinach and Swiss chard in mid to late spring; thin the seedlings to leave spinach 3in (7.5cm) apart, and Swiss chard 12in (30cm) apart. Start picking outside leaves as soon as they are big enough to use, leaving the rest of the plant to grow on. Spinach will bolt rapidly as the temperature rises, and must be re-sown regularly, but one sowing of Swiss chard should last all season. (In potagers, containers, or ornamental kitchen gardens, grow the red-stemmed variety known as rhubarb, or ruby chard, which tastes just as good, but looks more decorative.) Oriental greens need warm weather if they are to grow well – low temperatures will cause them to bolt early – so don't sow them until mid summer. Harvest whole plants as soon as they are large enough, and when they have formed tight hearts. Cook them in stir-fries.

Tomatoes

*A*mong the many varieties of tomatoes available today are some that remain green when they are ripe, and others that ripen to a creamy, or pale-yellow colour, described as 'white' in seed catalogues. You will also find striped tomatoes, yellow tomatoes, tiny, bite-sized cherry tomatoes, and giant, beefsteak tomatoes. Large tomatoes take longer to ripen than standard varieties, and cherry tomatoes need less water. Taste several varieties to find which you prefer before you decide which to grow. Tomatoes need rich soil with lots of humus, and plenty of warmth and sunlight. (A greenhouse gives a longer picking season in cool climates.) Space the plants 2ft (60cm) apart, and support them with stakes. Remove sideshoots from all but bush varieties to encourage heavier cropping. Feed regularly with a high-potash liquid tomato fertiliser, or an organic one, such as comfrey liquid and leave the fruits on the vines until they have ripened completely, and developed their full flavour.

Peppers and Aubergines

*P*eppers and aubergines are short, bushy plants that produce prolific crops continuously from mid to late summer.
They need the same care as tomatoes, but prefer a higher
temperature – a greenhouse is essential in all but the
warmest climates. There is no need to remove sideshoots,
but each plant should be tied to a short stake for support.
The stems of pepper plants are brittle, and snap easily, and
aubergine stems are very prickly, which makes it difficult to
harvest the fruits. You can pick aubergines and green peppers as soon as they are big enough to use, but if you want
red peppers, leave green ones on the plant to
ripen – this takes about 6 weeks, and the
plants will not set more fruits while they
are ripening. Grown outside the
crops are relatively trouble free
but when grown undercover
aphids, whitefly and red spider
can present problems.

Beans

*B*eans come in an incredible number of varieties. Some grow only 1ft (30cm) high, need no support, and quickly produce a tasty crop. Pole beans take longer to start cropping, because they need to grow up poles or netting first, but they produce beans over a longer period. Some beans are best eaten fresh, while others can be dried and stored for cooking in winter soups and stews. (This group incudes some of the best heritage varieties.) As a general rule, sow seeds 1in (2.5cm) deep, or set out young, pot-grown plants when all danger of frost is past. If beans fail to 'set', suspect cold weather, birds pecking off the flower buds, or dry conditions – spray the flowers with water every day in dry weather and soak the roots well.

Peas

Peas look great growing in my garden, but picking and podding them seems to take forever - and what I get in the pan sometimes makes me wonder if it was all worthwhile. If that is how you feel, then grow sugar snap peas, whose pods are eaten whole, thus dispensing with the time-consuming task of shelling. Either sow seeds in situ, 1in (2.5cm) deep, or − especially where rodents or soil pests are a problem − sow indoors in trays and plant out when the seedlings are a few inches (centimetres) high. Grow peas in neutral to alkaline soil, 3in (7.5cm) apart in triple rows with a 3ft (1m) wide path between them and the neighbouring crop. Push 4ft (1.2m) long twiggy sticks into the ground beside the plants so they can support themselves with their tendrils. When flowers appear, spray against maggots, and when the first pods are visible, cover the plants with netting to protect them from birds. Pick the pods while they are still young, tender, and tasty − don't wait for them to grow large and fat − they will not taste so good. To harvest peas for drying, pull up the plants and hang in a dry, airy place until the pods are brittle.

Sweetcorn

As well as needing a long growing season sweetcorn needs a large area in which to grow, but it is worth every bit of the space which it occupies. The taste of shop-bought cobs can't compare with the flavour of those picked from the garden and put straight into the cooking pot. As soon as the cobs have been picked, their sugars begin to turn to starch and the flavour is quickly impaired. Sow seeds ½in (1.5cm) deep in late spring. (In cold regions, sow in pots under glass and plant out in early summer, after the last frosts.) Corn plants are pollinated by wind, so sow or plant in large, square blocks, instead of rows, and space the plants 18in (45cm) apart each way. That way, each plant has several neighbours to ensure good pollination – expect about two cobs per plant. Water well in dry weather, and tap the flower tassels to help pollination. The cobs are ready when the kernels are creamy gold in colour, and squirt milky juice when pressed with a fingernail – peel back part of the green husk to test them. Pick, and cook them straight away. Harvest 'mini-corn' when the cobs of standard cultivars are miniature (approximately 3in (7.5cm) long).

Root Vegetables

*H*ome-grown root vegetables are delicious, particularly when they are grown organically. Carrots do not have that usual 'soapy' taint, and beets taste sweet and juicy. Besides the well-known varieties such as turnips, swedes, parsnips, radishes and Jerusalem artichokes, try the more unusual roots, such as salsify, scorzonera, and Hamburg parsley, which are real gourmet treats. Root vegetables need the right conditions if they are to grow well. If the soil contains too much nitrogen, they will fork, and be difficult to peel. Stony soil causes them to bend and twist to avoid the obstructions. Deep, light soil is best, and it should have been well-manured before the previous crop was grown. Root crops don't transplant well, so it's best to sow them in situ. Space the rows 12in (30cm) apart. When the seedlings emerge, thin them out to 1in (2.5cm) apart, then to 3in (7.5cm) for carrots, and 6in (15cm) for salsify and scorzonera. Sow seeds the same year that you buy them. Never allow the soil to dry out while the seeds are germinating.

Potatoes

Some gardeners believe it isn't worth growing their own potatoes, because they are so cheap to buy, but there is one good reason to do so – flavour. Choose varieties bred for taste, rather than commercial yields, and opt for early varieties; their flavour, when lifted straight from the garden, and cooked with mint and butter, is second-to-none. Potatoes are very easy to grow. Plant tubers 5in (12.5cm) deep. Space early varieties 12in (30cm) apart, in rows 24in (60cm) apart, and main-crop varieties 15in (45cm) apart in rows 30in (75cm) apart. In deep beds, plant earlies 15in (38cm) apart each way, and main-crops 24in (60cm) apart each way. As the stems appear, gently hill them up by drawing soil around them with a rake. Do this several times in early summer, until the foliage meets between the rows. Lift new potatoes when the first tubers are big enough to use (feel around in the soil to find out). Lift only as many as you need, and leave the rest to grow on. Leave second-early potatoes in the ground until the plants begin to flower, then lift them as you need them. Main-crop potatoes should be left in the ground until the end of the season, then lifted and stored for winter use.

First-early cultivars: 'Concorde', 'Epicure', 'Dunluce'
Second-early cultivars: 'Estima', 'Wilja', 'Marfona'
Main-crop cultivars: 'Navan', 'Maris Piper', 'Kondor'

Jerusalem Artichokes

Jerusalem artichokes grow 10ft (3m) tall and look just like sunflowers during the summer, but in autumn the plants are pulled up to reveal a harvest of knobbly tubers underneath. These tubers are cooked like potatoes, and can be boiled, baked, fried, or roasted. Very knobbly kinds are difficult to clean for cooking, but new varieties have smoother tubers that are easily scrubbed. The flavour is unique – you either like it, or you don't – and the texture is strangely waxy. They are one of the most easily grown vegetables, and very productive. Plant in early spring in a sunny spot in any but very poor, or waterlogged soil. Apart from weeding, you can ignore them all summer, then dig up the crop in late autumn. Store in a cool, dry place, and save some to replant the following spring. Plants are wind-proof – a row makes a good windbreak, or a decorative screen and their fibrous root system makes it a valuable pioneer crop on heavy ground.

Cucumbers

Nowadays, even if you don't have a greenhouse, it is possible to grow good cucumbers in cooler regions, if you choose modern outdoor varieties – they are as good as the indoor kind. To raise your own plants, sow seeds in a heated propagator at 70-80°F (21-27°C). Gradually lower the heat after the seedlings appear, to accustom them to colder conditions before planting them out. Alternatively, you can buy plants and set them out in the garden. Plant indoor cucumbers in an unheated greenhouse in late spring, and outdoor varieties in the open in early summer, well after the last frosts. Plant on a small mound of soil, and always water around the base of the mound, to avoid neck rot, which can kill young plants. Water sparingly at first, but increase both watering and liquid feeding (use tomato fertiliser) as growth speeds up. Tie stems to stakes for support. All-female varieties are easier to grow, and more productive. Cucumbers grow straight from the main stem of the plant. Remove sideshoots and tendrils, but take care not to break off flowers – baby cucumbers develop behind these when the petals are over. Cut cucumbers as soon as they fill out.

Melons

Melon plants are almost identical to those of cucumbers, and are cultivated in exactly the same way. Cantaloupes are best suited to outdoor temperatures, as they ripen quickly. In cold regions, plants produce more fruits if they are grown in a cold frame or greenhouse. Train the plants up canes in a greenhouse, and let them run over the ground in a cold frame. In the open, let them run over the ground, or put up a low netting 'fence' for them to climb over, to keep the fruits clear of the soil. The flowers need to be pollinated in order to set fruit. Outdoors, if there are plenty of bees around, they will do the job, but you will need to hand-pollinate plants under glass. Pick off a fully open male flower, remove the petals, and dab the flower into the centre of a female flower. (They have an embryo melon behind the petals.) Leave the melons on the vine until they are completely ripe, and have a musky scent. Test for ripeness by gently pressing the tip of the fruit around the old flower scar, with your thumbs. If it yields slightly, the melon is ready to eat.

Squash

*T*he squash family is a diverse group of fast growing vegetables that thrive in warm temperatures.
Summer squash include marrows, courgettes;
winter varieties include pumpkins and gourds.
Squash are good vegetables to interest children in
gardening. The plants grow so quickly you can
almost see the fruits swell. Depending on variety,
they have bright red, blue, or gold rinds, often
decorated with blotches, speckles, or stripes.

Sow the seeds in late spring, after the last frosts, in rich soil, or on top of the compost heap. Feed the plants regularly with liquid tomato fertiliser, and watch them take off. Pick summer squash, including courgettes, when they are large enough to eat – the more you pick, the more you will get. Leave winter squash on the vine to ripen in autumn, but bring under cover before the first frost. Store them in a cool room, or a frost-free shed or garage until you need them.

Salad Crops

Lettuces are the best-known salad crop. There are regular hearting kinds, crisp-hearted varieties, and upright cos lettuces. Red or green frilly types, and oak-leaved varieties do not form hearts – just cut a loose head of leaves when the plants are large enough. With 'cut-and-come-again' lettuces, you can pick leaves as you need them, and leave the rest on the plant to grow on. Apart from the 'cut-and-come-again' varieties, sow lettuce seeds little and often, for a continuous supply. They need light if they are to germinate, so barely cover them with soil, but keep them well watered, otherwise, they won't grow. Thin out the seedlings (don't try to transplant them in warm weather), to 12in (30cm) apart. Water the plants well in dry weather, and feed with a nitrogen-rich liquid fertiliser.

Salad leaves are the fastest things in the vegetable plot. They include rocket, lamb's lettuce (corn salad), sorrel, and purslane. Other leafy crops, such as chicory, endive, and spinach, can be harvested young, as baby leaves. For really creative salads, grow several types at the same time, or thinly sow a mixture of any of these, plus lettuce seeds, and snip the seedlings when they are a few inches (centimetres) high. (This mixture can also be grown on a sunny windowsill indoors in winter.) Grow salad leaves in the same way as lettuces; they don't form hearts, and can be grown 1-2in (2.5-5cm) apart. To ensure a constant supply, sow little and often – about every two weeks.

Mushrooms

Victorian gardeners grew mushrooms in pretty containers and brought them indoors for table decorations. The traditional way of growing them was very hit-and-miss, involving mushroom spawn on the lawn, or piles of fermenting manure whose temperature had to be taken regularly. Nowadays, mushroom growing is simplicity itself. You can buy a kit containing ready-spawned blocks of compost, which come complete with growing instructions. Kept in the dark at room temperature, a good crop of mushrooms should appear within a few weeks. With luck, the value of the crop will almost equal the price of the kit. All kinds of mushrooms, including the more exotic types, such as shiitake, are available, and make fascinating growing.

Herbs

The most popular culinary herbs are chives, French tarragon, marjoram, mint, parsley, rosemary, sage, and thyme; all have robust flavours, and, with the exception of French tarragon, are hardy plants that can live outdoors all year round, even in cooler regions. (Parsley is a biennial, but new plants should be grown every spring.) As a useful 'second string' you could include herbs, such as basil, chervil, summer savoury and dill. Chervil and summer savoury are hardy, but basil can't be put outdoors until after the last frost.

Herbs with an oriental flavour are fashionable now, too; try cinnamon or lemon basil, coriander, and lemon grass. Plant herbs in geometric patterns in formal herb gardens, use for edging a potager, or plant a mixture in a row in a kitchen garden. Most herbs except basil are robust and can survive most soil conditions and situations. However, they will not survive in waterlogged soils or in heavy shade. To stop invasive kinds, such as mint and horseradish, from spreading, grow them in large pots sunk up to their rims in the garden. Most herbs grow well in containers; grow a group in a large planter, or mix with small, edible flowers.

Baby Vegetables

These tiny vegetables are not special dwarf varieties, but simply normal vegetables that have been specially bred to develop a mature shape while they are still young and small. You can grow baby vegetables in the same way as normal varieties, but give them the best possible growing conditions – good fertile soil, and regular feeding and watering, to help them develop quickly. Because they are harvested when they are small, you can grow them closer together than conventional crops – about half the normal spacing for lettuces and spinach, and 2in (5cm) apart for carrots, kohl rabi, and other root vegetables. Baby leeks must be grown 1in (2.5cm) apart if they are to develop the characteristic slim, pencil shape, but the plants that produce baby zucchini and sweet corn are full-sized – it's only the fruits that are small, so plant them at normal spacings. Pick baby vegetables as soon as they reach the required size, otherwise they will continue to swell. Because they take up less space, they are ideal for very intensive growing methods, such as deep beds, containers, and potagers.

Edible Flowers

Edible flowers make pretty additions to salads, and good garnishes and table decorations. Suitable kinds to use whole include borage, English violets, nasturtiums, and primroses. Separate the florets of lavender flowers, and pull the petals from pot marigolds, daisies, and chive flowers. All of these can be picked from the garden, or grown for extra decoration among salad crops anywhere where they will not be swamped by vegetation. Edible flowers can be frozen in cubes of ice, or crystallised to make cake decorations.

CHAPTER THREE
Growing Know-How
Fruit

*F*ruit trees and bushes need a sunny, sheltered site, facing away from the early morning sun. Otherwise, in spring, when the trees are in blossom, early sun can scorch frosted petals. If this happens, the flowers will not be visited by pollinating insects, and the trees will not produce fruits. The soil should be deep, fertile, and well drained. Before planting, dig deeply, mixing in plenty of well-rotted garden compost, manure, or other organic matter, and some general fertiliser. If you want to train fruit trees against a wall, put up trellises, or wall nails and wires to support them, before planting. Cane fruits, such as blackberries and loganberries, need posts and horizontal wires to support them. Every spring, sprinkle some general fertiliser around the plants, and mulch the ground thickly. A high-potash feed in late summer is also beneficial.

Apples and Pears

*A*pples and pears are the easiest fruit trees to grow. A young tree bought from a nursery will have been trained into shape. Choose one grown on a dwarfing rootstock, if you want it to remain compact and to start fruiting within a few years. Unless there are plenty of fruit trees growing in your area, you will need to grow two different varieties that are capable of cross-pollinating to be sure of getting fruit. Ask your nursery or garden centre to suggest compatible varieties. If you want to plant your fruit trees in grass, leave a circle of bare earth 3ft (1m) in diameter around the bases of the trunks so that the young trees don't have to compete with the grass for water and nutrients. In winter, when the trees have lost their leaves, prune to thin out crowded shoots, and to keep the centre of the tree open. The branches should form a goblet shape. Cut out dead, diseased, and damaged shoots whenever they appear. If space is very short, choose a family tree, which has several different varieties grafted onto one trunk. Both dessert and cooking apples can be produced on the same tree, and they will all pollinate one another.

Cherries and Plums

The dwarfing rootstocks available for cherry and plum trees have less effect on the ultimate size of the trees than do those for apples and pears, so be prepared for these trees to grow to a height of at least 15ft (4.5m), and almost as much across. Expect them to take five years before they begin to produce reasonable crops. Buy well-shaped trees with several strong branches evenly spaced around their trunks. Most cherries and plums need cross-pollinating, but some are self-fertile. If you have room for only one tree in your garden, ask at your nursery or garden centre for advice on the best variety to choose. Plant the tree, allowing plenty of room for it to grow. Tie it to a stake for support, and leave bare earth around the base of the trunk for the first five years – after that, you can allow grass to grow up to the trunk, and underplant with spring bulbs, if you like. If you bought a well-shaped tree, the only pruning you will need to do will be to cut out any dead, diseased, and dying shoots whenever you see them. When the fruits are still green, drape the trees with netting to protect them from birds, and leave them to ripen fully before you pick them.

Containerised Fruit Trees

Dwarf fruit trees in pots make good plants for a patio. Choose naturally compact trees. Patio peaches are perfect; these are genetic dwarfs, with pretty blossom and full-sized fruits. Apple trees which have been trained as bushes on dwarfing rootstocks, small standard trees, or upright cordons, are also good. With the exception of fig trees, most other fruit trees are too vigorous to be happy in containers for long. Containerised figs can be grown as either bushes or standard trees, but they must be fed and well watered in summer to prevent fruit drop. Containers for fruit trees should be at least 18in (45cm) in diameter. Fill them with good, soil-based potting mix, water copiously in spring and summer, and feed weekly with a liquid tomato fertiliser – potted trees shed their fruits if their roots go short of moisture. In autumn and winter, water only when the growing medium looks dry, and protect plants from wind and excess wet. In severe weather, the roots of containerised trees may freeze in their pots – protect them by wrapping the containers in bubble plastic, or plunge them up to their rims in a garden bed. Alternatively, take them indoors.

Figs

Fig trees are naturally heat and drought tolerant once they are established, and are ideal for many 'problem' situations. They can be grown as bushes or trees, trained as fans against a wall, which is a good way of providing extra warmth and shelter for them in cooler regions, or grown in pots on the patio. Left unrestrained, a fig tree can grow huge. To keep it compact, and to increase its fruiting potential, you will need to confine its roots. Dig a hole 3ft (1m) square, line it with old bricks and rubble, then fill it with a mixture of good topsoil mixed with well-rotted compost, and plant into that. In cold regions, when the leaves fall, remove any partly grown figs, as they will not live through the winter, and may become infected. Prune the tree in late winter, when it is completely dormant – if you prune during the growing season it will bleed badly, and the sap loss may seriously weaken it. Leave the figs on the tree until the skins change colour, and the fruits feel slightly soft when squeezed.

Strawberries

You can grow strawberries spaced 1ft (30cm) apart each way in conventional beds, or in tubs, hanging baskets, or strawberry planters. Buy young plants in autumn or spring, plant them out straightaway, and keep them well watered. If you are growing them in beds, spread clean straw around the plants, or use strawberry mats, to keep the fruits clean and prevent mould. As the fruits swell, cover the plants with netting to protect them from birds. Raise the netting slightly above the plants on a framework of canes to prevent the birds from pecking through it, but make sure it is tucked well in around the plants, to stop birds from becoming trapped under-neath it.

Pick ripe fruits daily, and when the whole crop has been harvested, clip over the plants to remove old fruit stems and foliage, then sprinkle a high-potash fertiliser between them, and water it in. Keep containerised strawberries well watered, and feed them weekly with high-potash liquid tomato fertiliser. If you want early fruits, move the pots to the greenhouse in early spring.

Raspberries

Raspberries like lime-free soil – on alkaline soil they suffer from mineral deficiencies, but you can counteract these, to a certain extent, by feeding the bushes with sequestered iron in spring and summer. Summer-fruiting raspberries grow vigorously, and need lots of space. Prune them as soon as all the fruits have been picked. Cut all the stems that carried fruit to ground level, but leave the new shoots, which will carry next year's crop. Thin out excess canes, leaving the best 9in (23cm) apart. Tie these in to post-and-wire fencing for support. If time and space are short, grow autumn-fruiting varieties instead. These ripen in late summer and autumn. You can grow them in a bed, which means you get more fruit from less space. Birds are less likely to take the fruits but, in cold regions, the crop may be cut short by early frosts. Prune in early spring, by cutting all the canes down to ground level. The new shoots that grow in the summer will carry the new season's crop.

Gooseberries

Gooseberries grow on dense spiny bushes, which makes it difficult to pick the fruits. If you prune the plants so that the branches are spaced well apart, you'll get larger fruits, and they will be easier to pick. You will also reduce the risks of mildew by thinning out. Prune in winter when the bushes are leafless, and cut back new growth by half. Alternatively, grow them as cordons, and prune them in summer, cutting back all sideshoots to just beyond the point where the fruits are growing. Feed and mulch the bushes in spring, and keep them well watered when the fruits are swelling. You can pick gooseberries for cooking before they are fully developed, or use the trimmings from a large crop for fruit tarts. Leave dessert varieties on the bushes until they ripen in mid summer. The fruits are ready to eat when they have changed colour and feel slightly soft when squeezed.

Blueberries

On very acid soil, the only fruit that grows well is blue-berries. The bushes produce clusters of bell-like, white flowers in summer, followed by blue-black fruits with a powdery 'bloom'. In autumn, the foliage takes on fiery tints, and the plants are decorative enough to grow as ornamental shrubs. Yields are improved if two plants of different varieties are grown to cross-pollinate each other, but many varieties will set fruit even when grown alone. Blueberries need plenty of water during the growing season. If your garden soil is not suitable, you can grow them in pots. Use an ericaceous potting mix, and feed weekly with liquid tomato fertiliser, from early to late summer. The fruits are ready to pick as soon as they turn blue-black. Birds love them, so protect the plants with netting. You will need to pick the bushes several times as the berries ripen over a long period. Grow other heathland fruits, such as cranberries, in the same way.

Cane Fruits

Cane fruits include blackberries, loganberries, and other hybrid berries with similar growth habits. Most bushes are extremely prickly and, by growing them on post-and-wire supports, you can have a very secure, productive garden boundary. A few thornless varieties are available, but the flavour of the fruits can be inferior. Blackberries are not fussy about soil, and tolerate windy conditions well. All cane fruits are vigorous growers, and need heavy feeding. Canes soon become unmanageable unless they are trained, and you should tie all the shoots out horizontally in the same direction. During the summer, strong new sprouts grow out from the bases of the plants. Tie these up loosely and keep them upright. After the fruits have been picked, cut off all the old canes close to the bases of the plants and tie the new canes to the wires.

Blackcurrants

Blackcurrants are ideal fruits to grow on heavy, damp soil, and they will grow even more vigorously if the soil is rich in nutrients. Most blackcurrant bushes are large, but there are some small, modern varieties ('Ben Sarek') available that are perfect for smaller gardens. Keep the plants well watered when the fruits are swelling, and net the bushes to protect the fruits from birds. When the fruits turn black, snip off entire branches, and separate them later by drawing them through the prongs of a kitchen fork. Prune the bushes in winter; cut back a few old stems (no more than one fifth of the total) to ground level, or to the junction with a strong, young shoot. Bushes will crop on both old and young stems but more proficiently on new stems.

Red and Whitecurrants

Both these plants resemble small, upright blackcurrant bushes. You can grow them as bushes or cordons, and care for them in the same way as gooseberries. Redcurrants have a sharp taste, and can be made into a tangy jelly to serve with lamb or poultry. They are also delicious mixed with strawberries and eaten raw. In mixed-berry tarts they balance the sweetness of the other fruits. Whitecurrants are always eaten raw, and taste similar to grapes. They look pretty sprinkled into fruit salads. A mixture of redcurrants and whitecurrants makes a stylish garnish for cheeseboards and buffet tables.

Grapes

Grape vines make very decorative climbers on a wall or trellis, or over an arch or pergola. Grown in this way, they need no special treatment, but will still produce a reasonable crop. Tie the new growth in place to keep the plants tidy, and shorten long shoots and thin out surplus stems in winter. If you want a large crop for either dessert fruit or wine-making, the vines are best grown on post-and-wire supports with the stems trained out horizontally. Pruning can be complicated, so follow the illustrated directions you can find in specialist books. Vines need a very sunny spot and well-drained soil, with the addition of plenty of organic matter. Water during dry summers, as mildew can be troublesome if plants dry out.

Don't use fungicides on grapes intended for wine-making, as they may affect fermentation. Feed the vines with high-potash tomato fertiliser every week in summer. Thin out dessert grapes so that the bunches contain fewer, but larger grapes. Use narrow-nosed grape scissors to remove about one third of the fruits when they are slightly less than pea-sized. The tiny grapes can be used in fruit tarts. In cold regions, dessert grapes should be grown in a greenhouse.

Passion Fruit

Passion fruits grow on large, climbing plants, which have spectacular flowers of red, purple, or blue. The best species to grow for fruiting are *Passiflora edulis*, *P. quadrangularis* (the giant granadilla) and *P. mollisima* (banana passion fruit). They need plenty of warmth, so grow them in a heated greenhouse or conservatory in cool regions. Grow a single plant in a large pot to restrict the roots, and train the stems up over a trellis on a sunny wall, spreading them out well. It may take a year or two before the plant starts fruiting. Hand-pollinate the flowers with a small artist's brush. Each spring, prune the previous year's growth back to within 1in (2.5cm) of the main framework of branches.

Kiwis

Kiwis, or Chinese gooseberries, are brown, oval, slightly hairy fruits that are green inside. The plants are large, attractive climbers, which twine around trellises or poles for support. They will grow outside in all but the coldest regions, where they must be grown under glass, and heavily pruned and trained if they are to produce a crop. Outdoors, in a warm, sunny spot, they will produce some fruits, but not maximum yields. Male and female flowers are produced on separate plants, which are sold under different names, and you will need a male and a female to produce fruits. Varieties of *A. arguta*, which produce clusters of small, but delicious fruits, are self-fertile, so you need only one plant.

Citrus Fruits

Citrus fruits include grapefruits, lemons, oranges, and tangerines. There are also more unusual kinds, such as kumquats (small, oblong, orange-coloured, bitter-tasting fruits used in cocktails and preserves), oddities such as the variegated lemons (which have green and gold-patterned leaves, and striped fruits), and hybrids, such as the limequat, which is a cross between a kumquat and a lime. Citrus trees are evergreen and have strongly perfumed flowers, which often appear at the same time as the fruits. They need winter protection in cold regions, so grow them in pots and move them into a heated greenhouse or conservatory, where the temperature never drops below 50°F (10°C).

In summer, stand them out in a sunny, sheltered corner of the patio. The plants are happiest in lime-free soil, in containers just large enough to take their roots. Feed with liquid tomato fertiliser, and water freely in summer. Keep them on the dry side in winter. To taste their full flavour, allow the fruits to ripen on the plants, by which time the rinds should be well-coloured, and the fruits should yield slightly when squeezed.

Bananas

*B*ananas are the best-selling fruits in supermarkets, but probably the most difficult to grow at home, but it's fun to try if you can provide the right conditions. They need a temperature between 75 and 80°F (25°C), so a warm, sunny conservatory or greenhouse is essential. Choose a dwarf variety – *Musa cavendishii* produces yellow bananas, but the shorter *M. velutina* has red fruits. Plants are sometimes available from nurseries and garden centres, but you can grow them from seeds sown in individual pots and kept very warm after sowing. Banana plants make striking foliage plants, even if they do not bear fruit. If they do produce bananas, leave them on the bunches to ripen. After fruiting, cut down the whole stem and wait for a new one to grow – banana plants are herbaceous.

Trees from Seeds

When you bite into an exotic fruit from the super-market, do you ever wonder what its parent plant looks like? To find out, you can plant the seeds. Tropical fruits, such as avocado pears, dates, lychees, mangoes, and rambutans, will not survive a cold winter outside, but they make fascinating indoor plants. They are unlikely to produce fruits indoors, but they do have good foliage. Sow the seeds straight from the fruits – if they dry out, they rarely grow. Sow in potting mix, water well, then seal the pot inside a plastic bag. Stand it in a warm place out of direct sunlight – a windowsill above a radiator is fine. When the seeds germinate, take the pots out of the bags. The plants will grow quickly – in their natural surroundings, most grow into huge trees. Treat them like any tropical house plants.

Training Fruit Trees

Fan-trained trees are ideal for growing against a wall in cold regions. This is the perfect situation for warmth-loving trees, such as peaches and nectarines, or for accommodating plums and cherries when there is no room in the garden for a standard tree. Routine care involves cutting out stems that grow outwards, shortening the main branches when they grow too long, and tying in the new ones needed to continue the fan shape.

Cordon trees look more like broomsticks than trees, with fruit growing from clusters of short twigs. They can be grown 30in (75cm) apart, so you can fit several varieties into a small space. They are usually grown at an angle of 45°, which means that the top of a 9ft (2.5m) tree is only 5ft (1.5m) from the ground – a comfortable height for picking. A row of cordon trees make a good screen for dividing up a large garden, or for hiding eyesores. Put up a 5ft (1.5m) high fence of posts and horizontal wires, then plant the trees. Tie the trunk of each to a strong stake, and tie the stake to the support wires. Each year, in late summer, prune the sideshoots back to just above a cluster of developing fruits. Prune non-fruitful sideshoots to within 1in (2.5cm) of the current year's growth, which is soft and green. In winter, cut the top of the trunk back level with the top wire of your support fence.

Espaliers have three tiers of horizontal branches growing out from a central trunk, and can be grown either against a wall, or in the open with posts and wires supporting the branches. Each branch is pruned in the same way as a cordon tree. Fruits on espaliers ripen well, because they are not hidden by surrounding branches. Unless you fancy training fruit trees as a hobby, and can wait several years for the shape to develop, buy young, ready-trained trees from your nursery or garden centre.

Pruning

Pruning is the thing that worries most people who grow fruit. It is not absolutely essential to prune, but if you don't, the fruit will be small and poorly coloured. Pruning thins out branches and lets light and air circulate around the plant, helping the fruit to ripen well and colour properly. By reducing the number of branches, you reduce the amount of fruit the plant carries, so what is left receives more nutrients from the soil, and is bigger and of better quality. Unless you are an enthusiast, you need only thin out congested growth and cut out any dead, diseased, or damaged shoots.

A good pair of pruning shears is the most important piece of equipment for anyone who grows fruit. I find it useful to have two pairs – one for rough pruning and tidying, and a better-quality pair for precise work that needs a really sharp edge. There are two basic types of pruning shears – the more sophisticated (and more expensive), has two sharp blades which glide past each other with a scissor action. They give the best cut, and the blades can usually be removed for sharpening. The other type is known as anvil pruning shears. These have one blade that cuts down onto a rubber 'stop' or flat plate. They are excellent when new, but once the blade becomes blunt it can cause bruising to the stems. Some anvil pruning shears have a ratchet action which makes cutting through tough stems easier, and is ideal if you have weak wrists, or a touch of arthritis.

CHAPTER FOUR

Crop
Rotation

*Y*ou should avoid growing the same vegetables in the same bit of ground, year after year. Each crop takes up different nutrients from the soil, and each carries its own soil diseases, so the more often the crop is grown in the same spot, the more it depletes the soil of those nutrients, and the greater risk there is of soil-borne diseases building up.

*R*otation allows the crops to be grown in a different spot each year. First, the vegetables are divided up into three or four groups, then the vegetable garden is divided into the same number of plots. In the first year, grow one group on each patch, then move everything around one place the following year. That way, the soil is correctly treated for each crop in turn, and most problems are neatly avoided by good husbandry, rather than man-made remedies. Fruit, and other permanent crops, such as asparagus, which cannot be moved every year, are not included in the rotation.

Plot one should be heavily manured in autumn or winter; add a general fertiliser in spring, and grow peas and beans, which like plenty of organic matter, in this plot. These plants have nodules on their roots that 'fix' nitrogen from the air. After each crop, cut down the stems and leave the roots in the ground, where they will slowly release nitrogen into the soil to benefit the next crop.

Plot two should be lightly amended with well-rotted manure or compost in autumn or winter. If the soil is acid or neutral, apply lime to raise the pH to a little over 7. Apply a general fertiliser shortly before planting, and grow Brussels sprouts, cabbages, cauliflowers, broccoli, oriental vegetables, swedes, turnips and radishes on this plot.

Plot three should not be manured, but should be given a generous application of general fertiliser shortly before planting. If the soil is poor when you first start the rotation, you can improve it by digging in some completely decomposed organic matter, such as thoroughly rotted garden compost, coir, old potting mix, or the used contents of growing bags, in the autumn. This plot is for root crops, which fork or split if the soil contains too much nitrogen.

Plot one   *Plot three*

Plot two   *Plot four*

*I*n a traditional rotation, the entire fourth plot would be used for potatoes, but if you want to grow only a few rows, plant them in plot three, and use plot four for salad leaves, spinach and other leafy crops, and sweet corn and outdoor tomatoes. Prepare the soil in the same way as plot one. Alternatively, take this plot out of the rotation, and use it for perennial crops, such as asparagus and artichokes, or turn it into a herb garden.

*I*f crop rotation is not practical, either because your garden is very small, or the crops you want to grow don't fit in with the traditional cropping plan, simply compromise. Plant what you want, but avoid growing the same crop in the same place two years running. In autumn or winter, dig in organic matter everywhere except where you intend to grow root crops, but particularly where you will grow peas and beans. Always try to follow peas or beans with brassicas, so the brassicas can benefit from the extra nitrogen in the soil.

Catch-crops

However well-planned your kitchen garden, gaps will begin to appear from mid summer onwards, when crops, such as summer cabbages and over-wintering onions, are finished. Instead of leaving the spaces empty, use them for fast-maturing crops that will be ready before the end of the season. Suitable crops to sow up to mid summer include bush beans, lettuces, spinach, salad leaves, and early varieties of peas and carrots, which are faster growing than main crop varieties. In early autumn, plant spring cabbages, or onion sets for over-wintering.

Inter-cropping

Inter-cropping makes the most of every bit of space in a small kitchen garden. Sow or plant fast-maturing crops, particularly spinach, lettuces, and bush beans, between rows of slower-growing plants, such as sweet corn, main crop potatoes, and Brussels sprouts – the inter-cropped plants will be harvested by the time the foliage of the main crops covers the rows. This technique is only suitable for traditional kitchen gardens, where plants are grown at conventional wide spacings. On deep beds, the inter-cropped plants would be smothered by the foliage of the main crops. Vegetables maturing in under 12 weeks include beetroot, fennel, kohl rabi, summer lettuces and spring sown onions.

CHAPTER FIVE
Food for the Soil

Compost

Use healthy, green materials, such as lawn mowings, the outer leaves of vegetables, annual weeds, and kitchen scraps to make a compost heap. Don't use diseased plants and perennial weed, as you may spread spores or roots around the garden. Woody materials, such as tree prunings, take a long time to rot down, and need to be cut up finely, or put through a garden shredder before they are added to the heap. If you want good compost quickly, don't just pile the materials up in a heap – buy, or make compost bins. In an enclosed space, compost materials heat up fast, and in warm conditions the compost should be ready to use within 3 months. Construct containers from planks, and make them 3ft (1m) square and the same height. Leave 1in (2.5cm) gaps between the planks to allow air to get in, and make covers for the tops. Fill the first bin with alternate 6in (15cm) deep layers of lawn mowings, weeds, crop debris, and household waste. A mixture of materials is vital if you want well-textured compost which is neither slimy, nor too dry. Firm each layer down, damp it if necessary, and top it with a 1in (2.5cm) layer of garden soil or animal manure to hold in the moisture, and provide the natural bacteria and nitrogen needed to activate the heap. Continue building up the layers until the bin is full, then cover the top – a piece of old carpet makes good cover. Depending on the time of year, the compost will take 3–12 months before it is ready.

Worm Compost

A worm bin looks like a dustbin with a tap near the bottom. Its job is to make worm compost – an organic, soil-like substance, which is rich in nutrients and trace elements. To set up a wormery, put a layer of drainage material in the bottom of the container, cover it with some well-rotted compost, then add the worms (take some from your compost heap, or buy them in a fishing-tackle shop). Every day, add a layer of chopped, fresh, green material, such as kitchen waste, vegetable leaves, or weeds. The worms will digest the waste, and replace it with worm castings. When the container is full of compost, empty it, salvage the worms, and start again. Use the tap to drain off the liquid that is produced during the process, dilute it with water, and use it as a liquid fertiliser. Spread the worm compost around your vegetables.

Manure

Animal manures vary enormously in quality. Manure from intensive farms may contain chemical residues from foodstuff additives, and is best avoided. If possible, use manure from riding stables and organic farms, and stack it for a year, until it looks like fibrous compost, before you use it. Small amounts of fresh manure can be added to the compost heap as an accelerator.

Green Manure

Green manures are grown specially to dig into the soil to improve its texture. Suitable plants include agricultural lupins, alfalfa, mustard, and phacelia. These should be sown thickly any time during the growing season, then dug in before they flower. Sow grazing rye, tares, and field beans, which are particularly beneficial on clay soil, in late summer and leave them to stand through the winter, then dig them in six weeks before you want to plant or sow the plot. Green manure crops are easier to dig in if you cut them down and leave them to dry out first.

Seaweed

Seaweed is a useful bonus for gardeners who live near the coast, but obtain permission before gathering it. Avoid seaweed contaminated by oil, tar, or similar flotsam, and wash the fronds to remove salt, or lay them out on a gravel path for a few weeks in the rain.

Fresh seaweed can be dug in to the soil in the autumn, and will have decomposed by planting time. Alternatively, you can add it in layers to the compost heap. Seaweed is a good source of potash and trace elements, and inland gardeners can buy dried seaweed meal and liquid seaweed extract from organic garden suppliers.

Leaf Mould

*I*nstead of burning fallen leaves in autumn, convert them into valuable leaf mould. Pile them into a 'cage', made by tacking wire netting round four posts driven into the ground to make a square container. Dampen each load of leaves as you add them, and firm them down well. When the cage is full, cover the top with 1in (2.5cm) of soil. After about two years, the leaf mould should look fine and crumbly. Use it to mulch woodland plants, and as a substitute for peat.

Organic Granular and Liquid Fertilisers

$\mathcal{M}$any organic fertilisers and liquid feeds are available. If your local garden centre doesn't stock them, look in gardening magazines or directories to find the addresses of mail-order organic garden suppliers. Organic sources of nitrogen include hoof and horn meal and blood meal (dried blood). For phosphate, use bone meal (which is very slow acting) or rock phosphate. Organic sources of potash can sometimes be bought, but you can use wood ash from bonfires or wood-burning stoves. Fish, blood, and bone meal is a good general fertiliser, but it contains sulfate of potash, which is not truly organic. Liquid feeds made from fish or manure are available, and seaweed extract, worm compost, good-quality garden compost, and manure all provide valuable trace elements.

You can brew your own liquid plant food, made from comfrey. Special varieties of comfrey are sold by organic garden suppliers, but Russian comfrey (*Symphytum officinale*) is nearly as good. The roots of comfrey penetrate very deeply into the soil, and draw up minerals which are then stored in the leaves, which can be cut several times a year. Stand a water barrel (one that has a tap near the bottom), on some bricks to raise it high enough for you to fill a watering can from it. Fill the barrel with comfrey leaves, then top it up with water. Leave to brew for a month or so, then draw off the liquid, dilute it with an equal quantity of water, and use it to feed tomatoes and fruit. Use a weaker solution to feed other vegetables, and young, or less robust plants. When the barrel is empty, throw the comfrey on the compost heap, and start again. Always use liquid feeds, or soluble fertilisers diluted at the correct rate, to feed containerised plants – solid fertiliser is too concentrated and may scorch the roots. Liquid feeds are good for plants in greenhouse borders too. In the garden, use them when the ground is dry and solid fertilisers would not be dissolved, or whenever plants need a quick boost. Liquid fertilisers allow you to apply the appropriate nutrient when the plants need it. High-potash tomato fertilisers are good for all flowering plants, but dilute them to half or quarter the rate used for tomatoes. High-nitrogen fertilisers are best for foliage plants, and to give a quick boost to anything that is not growing well.

CHAPTER SIX

Doing the
Groundwork

Testing the Soil

One of the first things you should do when starting a kitchen garden is have the soil tested. A professional analysis can tell you how acid or alkaline your soil is (the pH value), and which nutrients it lacks, and what is needed to replenish them. Alternatively, you can buy a small soil-testing kit from the garden centre. If you think the soil pH may vary around the garden, make separate tests. Most vegetables do best around pH7, which is neutral – neither acid nor alkaline. Brassicas, peas, and fruits such as cherries and plums, prefer a slightly higher pH, while raspberries and blueberries need a lower pH.

Tools

Kitchen gardening doesn't need a lot of special equipment. In addition to the basic tools – a spade and fork for digging, a hoe for weeding, a rake for preparing the soil, and a trowel for planting – you will need a pair of good pruning shears, and a line to help get the rows straight when sowing or planting – you can make your own from two short stakes and a ball of string, or a wooden board marked into convenient planting distances such as 6in (15cm) and 1ft (30cm). Other useful items include stakes, bean poles and netting.

Paths

*G*ood paths make all the difference to a kitchen garden, and form part of the structure of ornamental gardens, such as potagers. Bare soil may look 'natural' but it soon turns to mud in wet weather, and quickly grows a covering of weeds, and grass paths need mowing, and may start balding if used overmuch. The best paths have hard surfaces, such as gravel or paving, laid over a foundation of hardcore. Gravel paths need to be edged with tiles, bricks, or planks of wood to stop the gravel spreading sideways into the beds.

Dealing with Perennial Weeds

Before you plant the kitchen garden, you will need to get rid of perennial weeds. These are recognised by their spreading root system or very deep tap roots and include ground elder, bindweed dandelion and couch grass. If you don't want to resort to chemical solutions, you can either sow grass, and keep the area mowed until no more perennial weeds come up, or cover the soil with black plastic, old carpet, or something similar, that will exclude the light. Both these methods can take two years or more, and may not be 100% effective. Alternatively, you can use a translocated weedkiller. This is a chemical that is taken in through the leaves, and moves inside the plant to the roots. It takes about six weeks to work.

Spading

Spading is the first step in preparing the soil. When making new beds, it is worth double digging. Dig a trench, one spade deep, and move the displaced soil to the other end of the plot. Fork organic matter into the base of the trench, then dig the next trench alongside, using the soil to fill the first one. Continue in this way across the plot, using the soil from the first trench to fill the last one. In future, it will be sufficient to spread organic matter over the surface of the plot, and turn it in with a fork or spade.

Preparing Deep Beds

Deep beds are very productive, and require very little work once they have been constructed, but they do take quite a bit of effort to make in the first place. First, mark out the area. The beds should be narrow enough to let you reach the middle from each side. Don't make them too long either, as you'll get tired of walking around them. Double dig the beds, adding as much well-rotted organic matter as possible, then never walk on them again, so the soil does not become compacted. Lay paved, or gravel paths between the beds for easy access. On water-logged, or clay soils, where deep cultivation is not practical, edge the beds with planks, and build up the soil to make raised beds instead.

Improving Clay Soil

*I*n wet weather, clay soil turns to mud, and in drought it sets hard and may even crack. The best way to improve clay is to dig in at least one bucketful of grit per square yard (metre). You will need to do this only once. The grit opens up the structure of the soil, aerating it and improving surface drainage. Every year, dig in as much organic matter as possible. If the soil is too wet in winter, do it in spring to avoid compacting the clay when it is wet.

Seeds

Most of the vegetable seeds sold today are of F1 hybrids. This means the variety has been produced by crossing two specific parents; the same cross has to be made again to get more seeds of the same variety. This explains why F1 seeds are so expensive, and why it is no good saving seeds from F1 hybrid plants – their progeny do not breed true. Since few new vegetable varieties are bred with the home-grower in mind, it is common to find 'commercial' characteristics, such as high yields, and pest and disease resistance, as features of F1 varieties. (The latter makes them ideal for organic growing, because the need to use insecticides and pesticides is reduced.) Modern varieties are also bred to crop all at once for easy harvesting; at home, this is fine if you grow for freezing, however, if you prefer to eat your vegetables fresh it's nice to be able to pick a little and often.

*T*he alternative to F1 hybrids is 'open-pollinated' varieties. These are older varieties that breed true from seed – heritage vegetables fall into this category – so you can save your own seed, which is not only a good way to cut down the cost of vegetable growing, but also enables you to grow rare varieties that are not easy to buy. Although the plants breed true from seed, insects may cross-pollinate them with other crops of the same type so, unless you are the only person in your area growing winter squash, for example, you should hand-pollinate them to be sure of getting the true variety. Using a small artist's brush, transfer pollen from a male flower to a female flower of the same variety, then tie a muslin or paper bag over a female flower. Wait until the petals fade before removing the bag, then label the developing fruit so you can distinguish it from others when you collect the seeds.

Preparing the Seed Bed

*I*f you sow vegetable seeds into rough, lumpy, or stony soil, many of them will not germinate. Choose a sheltered spot where the soil has been well culti-vated previously, and make a seed bed. Dig over the bed, removing weeds as you go, but don't add any organic matter unless it is so thoroughly rotted it resembles soil. Rake the surface to remove stones, roots, or other debris, then sprinkle with general fertiliser. Continue raking until the soil resembles cake crumbs. You now have a fine tilth, which is ready to be sown.

Sowing Outdoors

When your seed bed is ready, use a garden line to mark out a straight row, then draw the back of a hoe blade along the edge of the line to make a drill about ½in (1.5cm) deep for small seeds, or 1in (2.5cm) deep for larger ones. Sprinkle small seeds very thinly along the drill, and space larger ones individually, then rake the soil very gently to just cover them. On heavy clay soil, where seeds often rot, or light, sandy soil, where seedlings can dry out very quickly, you can improve the germination rate by sprinkling ¼in (0.5cm) of vermiculite along the drills before you sow, and using more of the same to cover the seeds. Keep seeds and the seedlings well watered.

Thinning and Transplanting

Vegetable seedlings come up quite thickly when sown in rows. You won't need all the plants, so wait until they are large enough to handle, then thin them out, leaving the strongest about 1in (2.5cm) apart. By the time the plants are 2-4in (5-10cm) tall, depending on what you are growing, they will be ready to transplant into their final positions in the garden. Prepare the planting site, then use a hand fork to dig up each seedling, taking care not to damage its roots. Dig a hole with the trowel, and holding it by a leaf, lower the seedling in place and spread out the roots. Adjust the height so the lower leaves are just above soil level, then fill around the roots with soil and water well.

Sowing Under Glass

 In cooler areas, if you want to grow frost-tender plants, or if you want early crops of hardy ones, you can raise the seedlings in a greenhouse, or on a warm, sunny windowsill indoors. Loosely fill clean trays with potting mix, and firm it lightly. Water well, then scatter the seeds very thinly on top. Sieve a little more potting mix over the top, to barely cover them. Place the trays in a well-lit place out of direct sunlight, until the seeds germinate, taking care not to let the growing medium dry out.

Sowing in Pots

Large seeds are easy to handle, and germinate quickly. You can cut out a lot of work by sowing them individually in small pots. Fill the pots with potting mix, and push one seed into each pot, until it is buried to roughly its own depth. Water well, and stand in a warm place, out of direct sunlight. When the seedlings are 3-4in (7.5-10cm) high, and the pots are filled with roots, harden them off and plant them out.

Multi-seeding

If you are short of propagating space, try multi-seeding. Sow several seeds in each pot of potting mix, and raise them under cover. This method is suitable for growing plants, such as onions, leeks, cabbages, salad leaves, and herbs, all of which have small seeds. When the seedlings come up, weed out the weakest to leave three or four to grow on. When the pots are full of roots, harden off the plants, then plant them out, still in their clumps, but at 2-3 times the usual spacings – they will reach normal size, and produce normal crops.

Pricking Out

When seedlings first come up, they each have a pair of baby 'seed leaves'. By the time they have one or two true leaves as well, they need more space. Prepare a new tray, and make a hole in the potting mix for each seedling. Use a dibber, or the tip of a pencil, to loosen the seedlings. Remove them one at a time, taking care not to damage the roots. Lift each seedling by holding a leaf, to avoid bruising the stem, and replant carefully in the new flat, spacing 1-2in (2.5-5cm) apart. Plant the seedlings with their bottom leaves just above soil level. Stand the trays in a well-lit place, and give just enough water to keep the potting mix evenly moist. When the plants are large enough, harden them off, then plant them out.

123

Propagators

If you raise many plants under cover, a heated propagator is a great help. It is best used on a greenhouse bench, or in a sun-room or conservatory, where there is an electric socket nearby. Most propagators need a layer of damp sand in the base to distribute the heat, but some have a heated 'blanket', which should be kept dry. Switch the heat on a few days before you intend to sow, and set the thermostat, if there is one, to the appropriate temperature. Sow and water the pots or flats, place them in the propagator, and leave them until the seedlings are large enough to prick out. When you have pricked them out, return the seedlings to the propagator for a few days to help them recover, then gradually reduce the heat to acclimatise them to outside conditions. When you remove them from the propagator, put them in a warm humid place with diffuse light for a few days, as a sudden change in surroundings may set them back.

Hardening Off

Plants that have been started indoors must be hardened off for two or three weeks before they are planted out, to accustom them gradually to the colder, windier conditions outdoors. Harden them off in a cold frame, if you have one. Move the plants to the frame and keep the lid down at first, then raise it on fine days, and slowly increase the plants' exposure to the open air, until the lid is only closed at night. Finally, leave the lid up at night too, except when cold weather is forecast. If you don't have a cold frame, stand the plants outside in the garden on fine days, bringing them back in at night until the weather is warm enough to plant them out safely in the garden.

Planting Out

While the plants are hardening off, prepare the soil where they will be planted. Rake in the fertiliser, and leave the surface level. (Firm the soil in the brassica bed by treading it with your heels before the final raking.) To plant the seedlings, use a trowel to dig a hole a little bigger than the pot, then up-end the pot, and tap the base sharply with the trowel. Keep the root-ball intact, and place the seedling in the hole so the top of the root-ball is slightly lower than the surrounding soil. Fill around the root-ball with soil and firm gently in place, leaving a shallow depression around the plant to aid watering. Keep well watered until they are established.

Follow-on Crops

During the growing season, there will be several changes of plants in the kitchen garden. As soon as you have harvested early crops of lettuces, spring cabbages, and potatoes, clear the ground, and put in the next crop as quickly as possible. There is no need to spade the soil again, but sprinkle some general fertiliser along the rows to replace nutrients, and fork over lightly. Rake well, then plant or sow.

Crop Protection

Horticultural fleece is the modern equivalent of cloches, and helps to extend the growing season by allowing plants to crop earlier in spring, and by keeping late crops safe from frosts in autumn. In spring, prepare the soil and cover it with black plastic to warm it up. Remove the plastic, and sow or plant as usual, then drape the fleece over the bed, and bury the edges in the soil, or use stones or bricks to hold it down. Leave it over the plants until the weather warms up, and the plants are growing well, but remove it in hot weather, or they may overheat. Towards the end of the season, when cold weather threatens, spread the covers over late crops, such as lettuces, baby carrots, and late peas, to keep them growing for as long as possible. Use them to protect late crops of frost-tender vegetables, such as bush beans, and zucchini, too.

Synthetic Mulches

If you want a totally weed-free kitchen garden, without doing any weeding, use black plastic. This may not look too good, but it certainly looks better than an overgrown patch of weeds. Use special slitted or perforated black plastic sold for the purpose. Unroll it over the ground after preparing the soil, stretch it out flat, and hold in place with wire pegs, or stones. Cut X-shapes in the plastic, peel back the flaps, plant through the holes, then tuck the flaps around the plants so no soil is exposed to light. Water, liquid feeds, and air can reach the soil through the tiny holes or slits, but few weeds will germinate, because the plastic excludes most of the light. Use a heavy-duty plastic for fruit trees, bushes, and other permanent crops, and a lightweight type for vegetables.

Planting Trees

Container-grown fruit trees and bushes can be planted at any time of year except when the ground is frozen, very muddy, or very dry, but autumn and spring are the best times to plant them, if you can. Dig a hole several times larger than the size of the pot, and mix plenty of well-rotted compost or manure in the bottom, then hammer in a stake to support the tree. If planting in spring, mix in some general fertiliser – in autumn, use bone meal. Remove the plant from its pot and place it in the hole. Check the level – the top of the root-ball should be flush with the surrounding soil. Adjust the level if necessary, then fill in around the roots with a mixture of soil, and compost or manure. Water the tree well, and secure it to the stake with a tree tie, which will not chafe the bark in windy weather. Bare-root trees must be planted straightaway, or the roots will dry out. Plant in the same way as container-grown plants, but spread the roots out in the bottom of the hole. To find the correct planting depth, look for the ring of soil on the trunk, and plant to that level.

Watering

Most vegetables need a great deal of water, so it's a good idea to equip the kitchen garden with a tap, especially if it is some distance from the house, and keep a hose and watering can handy. Newly planted vegetables need most water, but in a dry summer all crops need watering, or they will become tough and stringy, or run to seed. Fruit trees, canes and bushes need watering until they become established, but after that they can, for the most part, take care of themselves. In dry summers, it is worth watering soft fruits, particularly strawberries, while the fruits are swelling. When you water, do so very thoroughly, then wait until the plants need watering again – don't water little and often. Direct the water to the bases of the plants and let it soak in – don't sprinkle it over the surface – it will just evaporate. In hot weather, remember always to water in the evening so the plants have all night to take up the water before it evaporates.

131

Pests and Diseases

*N*owadays, few kitchen gardeners are keen to use chemical pesticides, both out of consideration for wildlife and the environment, and because they will be eating the produce themselves. As soon as you stop using pesticides, beneficial insects will begin to colonise the garden, and keep pest levels down. If you provide facilities to encourage beneficials, you will soon have a thriving population. They need places to over-winter, nectar for adults to feed on, and undisturbed areas in which to breed – a border of wildflowers around the garden will provide everything they need. For a more decorative effect, surround the garden with old-fashioned hardy annuals, or plant a herb garden, and leave dead stems untouched throughout the winter.

*T*here is nothing worse than spending months caring for a crop, only to find that a sudden plague of pests seems set to ruin it. When this happens, many gardeners resort to pesticides, because natural predators would be unable to remove the attackers in time. There is no need to spray the whole kitchen garden – treat only the plants that are affected, and use a specific aphicide that will control only the pest causing the problem. That way, beneficials will not be harmed. Avoid using systemic sprays on edible crops, because they remain active in the plants for a long time. Always follow the makers' instructions precisely, spray in the evening to avoid harming bees, and don't spray in windy weather, or onto open flowers. Do not eat, freeze or preserve sprayed crops until after the interval indicated on the product label, which may vary from one day to two weeks, depending on the product.

*Y*ou can protect plants from harmful pests with
fine-mesh netting, which is sold by mail-order
organic garden suppliers, and garden centres. Use
the netting to cover seedbeds, or young plants. Tuck
it around and under the plants – tie it around the
bases of brassica stems – and leave it in place
throughout the life of the crop. Check that the plants
are not harbouring pests before you cover them, or
the pests will breed inside the mesh. In the greenhouse, use biological controls
to protect plants, or stand
pots outside for a few
weeks to clear outbreaks
without spraying.

If growing conditions are good, vegetables rarely suffer from problems. 'Good growing conditions' means
that the soil and situation are right, and
the plants are regularly fed and watered to
keep them growing steadily, without setbacks. When
plants are placed under stress, pests and diseases can become serious problems. Often, there
is no need to use chemicals if they are caught in
time. Small infestations of aphids,
caterpillars, or other pests can
be removed by hand.

CHAPTER SEVEN

Reaping the Benefits

Dealing with Gluts

However well you plan the kitchen garden, sooner or later you will get a glut of something. Usually, you will be able to freeze the surplus, but some vegetables, lettuces and cucumbers for example, don't freeze successfully. To avoid wasting them, cook them in dishes that make good use of large amounts of produce. Surplus lettuces can be cooked with green peas, or used like spinach, and you can grate cucumbers into plain Greek yoghurt to make tzatziki to accompany kebabs, or to use as a dip with Indian food.

Freezing is the most reliable way of storing surplus crops. If you are in a hurry, you can freeze prepared fruits and vegetables without blanching, but the storage time will be reduced. This is also a good way to prevent gluts of fruit from becoming over-ripe, when you do not have time to make jam or wine immediately. My favourite way of using up gluts of tomatoes, peppers, and aubergines is to make ratatouille, which freezes much more successfully than the ingredients do if frozen separately before they are cooked.

Vegetables

Where possible, leave main-crop roots, such as potatoes and carrots, in the ground, and dig them up as you need them. Once frosts threaten, dig them up, spread them out to dry without washing them (they keep for longer if left dirty), then store them in paper sacks in a frost-free shed or garage, or in a root cellar. Winter-hardy crops, such as Savoy cabbages, Brussels sprouts, and leeks, are best left in the ground and harvested when you need them. Surplus summer roots and brassicas are best frozen. Blanch and skin tomatoes, or make them into a purée before freezing. Cut peppers and aubergines into chunks, or make them into prepared dishes. Salad crops, such as lettuces, can't be frozen, but oriental vegetables and spinach can.

Herbs

*H*erbs can be preserved by chopping and freezing in ice cube containers with a teaspoonful of water, but drying is more convenient for large quantities. Gather herbs before they start flowering, and wash them only if absolutely necessary. If you have the space, spread them out on drying racks. Otherwise, hang them upside down in a warm, shady, well-ventilated place. You can peg small bunches to a drying rack on the kitchen ceiling for decoration, but never dry herbs for culinary use in a room where temperatures fluctuate, or where vapour gathers. When the leaves are completely dry, but still green, remove them carefully from the stems, and store in dark-coloured glass jars.

Fruit

Soft fruits don't ripen all at once – you can pick over the same bushes, canes, or strawberry plants for several weeks, and find ripe fruits almost daily. Most soft fruits are best eaten straightaway, or cooked the same day. Refrigerate them immediately after picking, and freeze surplus crops. Eat plums and cherries straight from the tree, or use them for cooking or making jams. Any surplus can be frozen, and used for cooking later. Early-ripening varieties of apples and pears should not be stored. Eat early apples straight from the tree, and pick pears and bring them into a warm room for a few days, until they are soft and ready to eat. Pick late-ripening apples and pears in autumn, before gales blow them down. Select only perfect ones to store, to avoid rotting. They will keep for a few weeks in the salad compartment of the fridge, or you can pack them in plastic bags, which have a few air holes, and store them in a cool shed or garage for 6-8 weeks. For longer storage, lay the fruits out, not quite touching, on slatted shelves in a shed or storeroom with a constant temperature of 45-50°F (7-10°C).

Published by MQ Publications Limited
254-258 Goswell Road, London EC1V 7RL

Copyright © MQ Publications Limited 1999
Text © Sue Phillips
Illustrations © Anny Evason

ISBN: 1 84072 137 5

1 3 5 7 9 8 6 4 2

Printed and bound in Hong Kong